Man-Snatcher

How to Make Her Man Yours

Jeanine Michelle

authorHOUSE®

AuthorHouse™
1663 Liberty Drive
Bloomington, IN 47403
www.authorhouse.com
Phone: 1-800-839-8640

First published by AuthorHouse 3/1/2010

ISBN: 978-1-4490-7619-1 (e)
ISBN: 978-1-4490-7618-4 (sc)

Printed in the United States of America
Bloomington, Indiana

This book is printed on acid-free paper.

This book is dedicated to Ann Summers

Thank you for always believing in me and for teaching me that anything is possible when you have a plan and a dream with money being the last thing to worry about! Thank you for being my "cheerleader" and I hope to one day be there for you as you have always been there for me!

Jeanine

Acknowledgements

Many thanks to everyone that has been supportive in helping me in the final creation of <u>Man-Snatcher</u>.

Special thanks to my sister Brittany who has truly been the wind beneath my wings these past two years, Cristal who I consider not only my cousin but my friend, Aunt Larraine who only wants to see me smile as a mother would, my brother Larry who has been more helpful than words can say, Arrie who has taught me no matter what, it can be done and Bobby who encouraged the laughs…HA! And Daddy…1 Book!

Also, I want to "Thank" my book club team: Brenda, Barbara, Rosalind, Gena, Noreen,Tasha, Katelyn and Sheena. Without all of you, I could not have developed this female fueled book.

Last but not least, I can't forget my "eye-candy"… "04-24 made many lives wonderful!" No matter where life takes us both, I hope our friendship never ends!

XOXO

Jeanine Michelle

"If I told you that you would not fail at one thing
you chose to do -- what would you do?"

Dear Friend,

Before you can make "her" man "your" man, you <u>must</u> be able to answer **"YES"** to <u>all</u> of the following questions:

1. Do you consider yourself sane?

2. Is this man NOT married?

3. Do you envision a future with this man?

4. Are you willing to share this man for 60 days?

5. Are you able to do late night drives past his house and accept her being there?

6. If you succeed at making him "your" man, will you be able to trust him?

If you have answered "Yes" to all of the questions above, then proceed in reading "Man-Snatcher"…

The book that teaches you how to make "her" man… YOURS!

GO GET YOUR MAN

Congratulations!

You are now on your way to becoming an official man-snatcher!

The next two months will be fun and enticing but they will also be very challenging with the end result being rewarding!

So sit back, buckle your seat belt as this book drives you to "your" man!

Introduction

For the past 19 years, I believed that you should never want anyone else's man. I believed we, as women, should stick together and respect one another and I religiously followed the saying:

"Do onto others as you would want them to do onto you"

However, over the past months, I have learned that you never know what your actions will be until you are placed in a real-life situation.

Ladies, here is my story...

I had just come out of a heart-breaking situation. I had lost the love of my life after 19 years. Not only was I lost, saddened and distraunt, "I WAS LONELY". But after a long ten months, I spotted my "eye-candy!"

Ladies... he was six-foot tall, caramel complexion with a muscular physique. And if that wasn't enough to be true...

he was personable! Yes, funny, charming and definitely a showstopper in my eyes!

But guess what -- **HE WAS TAKEN!**

Although this man was not married, he was in fact involved with a young lady that had been his support for two years.

So just like you, I was in a situation which required me to use my creativity in making "her" man... MINE! And after being successful, I decided to write a story to help guide females in getting the man they want and not settling for the man that wants them!

Contents

Chapter 1   1
   70 mph

Chapter 2   11
   One Thousand Four Hundred &
   Forty Hours = 60 Days!

Chapter 3   17
   Keep Your Red Shoes Polished!

Chapter 4   25
   Don't Be His Old Princess

Chapter 5   31
   Ice Cream, Cake & Cookies

Chapter 6   37
   Be Salsa! … Not a block of cheese

Chapter 1
70 mph

Now that you spotted your "eye-candy," what are you going to do to make him yours?

SIMPLE!

Just like a highway, you have four choices on which lane you will drive to making this man yours:

The shoulder?

> The slow lane??

> > The middle lane???

> > > **Or The fast lane!**

Which lane will you decide to take to make him yours?

Choice 1

"The Shoulder Lane"

The shoulder is a lane where nothing is happening. Well, at least nothing positive. Although you are welcomed to ride this lane, I strongly suggest **you do not!**

In this lane, your man will pass you by as you sit around admiring him by squealing like a teenager "oh-he is so fine!" and telling your girl-friends "Oh! I wish I could make him mine."

This lane is for those ladies that are shy and nervous about using their female creativity in getting the man they want and rather accepting the man who wants them.

If you choose to ride this lane, you will notice the highway will continue to move as you sit like a broken down car in the shoulder lane awaiting a tow truck to pull you away.

Choice 2

"The Slow Lane"

The slow lane is for you cautious ladies! In the slow lane you have made an attempt to go after your "eye-candy." But, unfortunately, you will not be successful. Although the initial interest was there, and yes you did spark this man's attention, unfortunately going this route will only get you a periodic call, random text and possibly one date.

The reason you cannot be successful in this lane is because you are too cautious! You are nervous to take the chance of switching lanes because you are worried about hidden obstacles that might develop in pursuing this man. So instead you decide to let him give you directions -- but only to find there is no destination in riding this lane.

So if you decide to ride this lane, I want you to think to think about this… What are your chances of getting a ticket in the slow lane?

Choice 3

"The Middle Lane"

The middle lane is for the girl that is patient yet wants a challenge! This lane requires you to set your cruise control. By setting your cruise control, you will be riding a nice, smooth pace to getting your man but there will be some braking which will cause obstacles.

If you decide to ride the middle lane, your relationship will develop only if the traffic is clear. This means if his lady gives him free time, you will be able to continue to ride straight to making him yours. If his lady requires a lot of his attention by acting like a cop on highway patrol, you will constantly have to brake and that will create obstacles in developing your relationship which will require you to constantly re-set your cruise control.

Although this lane has that potential to lead you home in the right direction -- just remember for every 30 miles forward on the highway, you encounter a reason to stop at a rest area and this will cause frustration in making her man "yours"!

Choice 4

"The Fast Lane"

If you want her man... you must do **70 MPH!**
Go in- Go in- Go in!

When you drive on a highway, you always notice the cars driving in the fast lane. You think to yourself that person must have an agenda since they are in such a rush. Correct! This is the lane you must ride to make him look at you above any other female.

The fast lane is the lane for anyone that wants to be successful at getting their "eye-candy." It is the lane for someone in control of the wheel by acting the role of who <u>she wants to be</u> and not the role of the passenger. If you want to be his lady... **You must act like you are his lady!**

So the question is how will you drive 70 MPH and get home safely?

1. Call him twice a day
2. Send him a sweet or supportive text twice a week
3. Plan a date each week
4. Become his "party friend"

The list is simple! You are probably wondering what I mean about becoming his party friend. Since most women feel they are second to a man's friend, why not become his friend too? Yes! Make everything you do together exciting. Show him you are fun and, most of all, stress-free. The twist to keeping him not looking at you as just one of his buddies is by creating guilt. Not by feeling guilty to her -- but to **YOU!** One evening I want you to drive past his house when you know his girl is there and beep your horn and then send him a text stating "I see you are busy!" He already knows that he is cheating on her and now he will feel guilt to you because you know he is with her. Remember you are playing the role of who you want to be.

So it is natural that you may start feeling like you are his weekend girl. Wonderful! Think about it… What are the best days you of the week?

Besides the weekend, I need for you to become his Wednesday night girl! Since the middle of the week needs excitement, I want for you to plan a date every Wednesday and make this night only about you and him… absolutely NO FRIENDS! Make this night spicy and I guarantee that you will be on his mind until your next evening out.

So remember when choosing which lane you will travel in making "her" man "yours," keep in mind that nothing good happens in the shoulder. You cannot get a ticket in the slow lane, the middle lane keeps braking and the only way to getting your eye-candy is by doing **70 mph.**

After reading this chapter how will you make him yours?

After reading this chapter how will you make him yours?

Chapter 2

One Thousand Four Hundred & Forty Hours = 60 Days!

In a period of 60 days, any man should know if they are truly interested in you or not. He should be almost ready to make a decision of whether he wants to keep developing what he has with you or if he wants to stay in his present relationship.

Realistically, no man is going to leave his girl after meeting you for one day or even for one week. But it is fair to say that he should have a stronger interest in you after one month -- whether it is in your best interest or not.

After 30 days, he should be thinking of you throughout the day and his relationship with her should begin to get rocky. This is when she becomes an annoying pain in his side and you need to be there ready to rub it out.

The next 30 days you must ride the highway as if the police were on strike. As you ride, I want you to pretend you read a billboard which read "Be Sexy, Be Sweet, Spoil him Rotten!" I want for you to memorize these words…For this is the secret recipe on how to make him yours over the next 30 days!

You need to be sexier than ever, sweeter than candy and you need to spoil him! Yes, I said "SPOIL HIM." Remember, no matter what a man's age or what his professional status may be, inside all men lives an adolescent boy with one major fan: His Mommy! And why do little boys love their mommy? Because Mommies spoil their little boys! So from this you need to find that special spot that tickles his heart and do what ever it takes to spoil this man!

Here is a suggestion of how to make him feel special:

1. Send him a card

This card <u>should</u> <u>not</u> be mushy or lengthy in words but rather something simple to let him know you were thinking about him. I want for you to **ONLY** sign your name. <u>Absolutely NO</u> <u>messages</u>.

You know us women we love to write messages and dot our "I" with hearts. At this point, I beg for you not to do this. I just want for you to purchase a playful card and sign your signature. So you are thinking why send him a card? Because we avoid mail. So think about how special you would feel to get a surprised card in the mail. Now you are probably wondering why only a signature? Simple! Men have egos and they feel that when women do nice things for them, it is because they are into them.

Yes, we want him to know we were thinking about him -- but we just don't want him to know how much. So when you only sign a card with a signature, it makes him question what type of vibe to take from your card.

As all of us ladies know... MEN LOVE A CHASE! Even though we know the role we are playing on how to make this man yours, he should not know your intentions at this point.

After reading this chapter how
will you make him yours?

After reading this chapter how will you make him yours?

Chapter 3

Keep Your Red Shoes Polished!

What do you think of when you see a red shoe?

1._____

2._____

3._____

4._____

5._____

Sexy Confident Showstopper

A lady needs to be like a red shoe and your "eye candy" should only see you polished. A man loves a well-kept women. So keeping your nails, toes, hair, make-up and clothing perfect is a must!

During the first 60 days, your man should never see you in the same outfit or the same shoes. Every time you have an encounter, you should be a showstopper! I want you to make it a point to always wear high heels! When Mattel made the most successful selling toy in the world they could have just made another baby doll but instead they made Barbie. A doll that would inspire vanity in every little girl. And what made Barbie extra special…her high heels!

Did you really think Barbie was made to stand on her tippy toes for no reason? As Oprah is the voice of America, Barbie is the epitome of a woman. Barbie stands on her toes to accentuate her curves. Over the years, even though Barbie has kept the same name and face, she has not faded with the trend due to her constantly changing her wardrobe and maintaining trendy images to stay with the times.

Unlike Barbie, we as women get comfortable in a relationship and we stop polishing our shoes. We begin walking around without make-up, forget to match our bra and panties, wear that new piece of lingerie called "the oversized tee-shirt", forget to put the finishing touches on our hair and keep the same old side part, curled under look.

Comfortable is the level his girl may be at -- **but not you**! If this means you must wear spanks, create flawless skin with make-up, wear stilettos after working an eight-hour day... so be it! You must do whatever it takes to appear perfect no matter how uncomfortable you may feel.
You do not buy a red shoe because it matches an outfit but instead you buy it because it is different. It creates attention and the person wearing it looks confident and dominant!

So if you treated yourself like a red shoe, how would your man feel when he is with you? He would feel **DAMN** GOOD! As you are getting ready for your date, I want for you to think about a red shoe and never be anything less than polished. Since men are competitive, I guarantee he will get an extra boost of confidence with you on his arm.

So it is easy to be polished when you are leaving from home, but how do you continue to stay perfect during an unexpected overnight stay? So here are two basic rules to never forget!

Rule #1

Never lose the look he just went out with! You can always turn up the sex appeal but never take off the make-up!

Rule #2

Always carry a toothbrush! Brush your teeth twice: before he kisses you good night and before he kisses you good morning!

Finally, the most important thing to focus on when keeping your red shoe polished is give him an impression that your look is not temporary. You must continue to keep that look that originally attracted him to you and kick it up two notches. Before you go out on a date, I want you to remember what you originally wrote for what you think of when you see a red shoe. Most of all -- never let him see you unpolished!

After reading this chapter how will you make him yours?

After reading this chapter how will you make him yours?

Chapter 4

Don't Be His Old Princess

Don't Be His Old Princess simply means: **Don't Be Her!**

Over the first couple of weeks while having conversations with this man, he will spurt out little things about his princess. Some things positive and some negative. This is the time when you need to clean out your ears with q-tips and become a very good listener. I want you to listen to everything—all the good and the bad! I want for you to take the good and look at those qualities and compare them to yourself and then I want you to take the negative comments and make sure you are not demonstrating them.

If he mentions that he **LOVES** her spaghetti, guess what, you never ever make him spaghetti! Why would you attempt to make him something when he has already given her the prize? There is no need to compete to make yours better because he has already used the four letter "**LOVE!**" At this point, you have learned you do not need to remind him of her. If you decide to compete and make your spaghetti, he will be thinking about hers and that is not what you want him to do.

Now it is time to listen to the negatives and accept his minor flaws. Meaning if she is complaining to him that she hates when he mixes his socks and underwear in the same drawer, I want for you to think if this is something you can live with.

So here is the trick to reeling him in:

You must be supportive of her! Yes, supportive of her! When he is talking about her complaints, I want you to see her view and give a neutral supportive response. At this point, he looks at you as a friend even though he does not know of your secret intention of snatching him from her.

The most important factor now is that you should be living your life as if she does not exist. Her name should <u>never</u> be brought up by you, and if he brings it up, you are to make it seem as though it does not phase you at the very least.

Men love powerful, confident women. So it is your goal to make him be more impressed with you than he is with her. Show him your best qualities, talk about your future goals, include him in on your work achievements and make your life seem exciting! This will definitely give you a feel by his reaction if he wants to include you in his future. For example: If your boss gives you a compliment at work about your work, let him know. You want him to see how much others admire you.

Show your independence! Ladies, this is a new century and we must get rid of the thoughts that a man should pay for everything! If you want a man to see your genuine interest in him, you must treat him to nice things too. I want for you to pay for the first date or at least offer! I promise this will make your "eye-candy" very impressed with you. But here is the cherry on the sundae: When you pick up the tab, you must only pay with a Benjamin (the $100 dollar bill!). Nothing is more impressive and dominating than when a person pays with a hundred dollar bill! For some reason, it makes people go from ordinary to extraordinary when a person pays with larger bills.

The key point in this chapter is that you need to make this man impressed with you. **If you are trying to make him leave her for you, why would you ever want to be her?** Most of all, you need to remember these two crucial things:

1. Her negative qualities: you need to possess the opposite

2. Her positive qualities: you need to do equally or better

3. If he uses the word "Love" -- don't do it at all!

So never ever be his old princess but rather become his new "Priceless Gem!"

After reading this chapter how will you make him yours?

After reading this chapter how will you make him yours?

Chapter 5

Ice Cream, Cake & Cookies

Ice Cream, Cake and Cookies…
(What do they all have in common?)

They are SWEET, SWEET, SWEET! Who doesn't have a sweet tooth? Your sweetness is what is going to win his heart. Having sweet qualities can make anyone seem more attractive.

Do you recall the movie "Dirty Dancing"? The character "Baby" was very simple whereby some viewers may have felt she was unattractive. As the movie line developed, her sweetness and kind heart made her appear more beautiful by the end of the movie. So this proves that a not-so-attractive person can become more attractive through their sweetness. Just as a beautiful person can become less attractive if they possess a nasty personality.

The most vital point to remember when reading this chapter is: Your man is currently involved in a relationship -- he does not need to be stressed out by another lady. So you must be like **SUGAR!** -- not only to him but to his family, friends, female friends and even ex-girlfriends.

Sweetness is the #1 priority when interacting with his family! Your presence with this man will be an awkward situation at first for everyone involved when he invites you to a family affair. It will be awkward for him because his family knows he has a lady and awkward for you because everyone will be looking at you wondering why he is with you.

Too overcome this, you must be confident and tell yourself "he must have some type of interest in you. Because if he didn't, he would not have brought you around." So when he invites you to meet his family, I want for you:

1. Put your red polished shoe forward

2. Address his parents as Mr. & Mrs. (never a first name)

3. Refer to your "eye-candy" as your friend

Let his parents see your intelligence through your choice of conversation topics and mannerisms. Let them admire you and be proud that their son is surrounding himself with mature, educated and positive people.

His friends will be a challenge within itself because they are all looking at you as just another one of his garden tools. So the best way to overcome this challenge is by becoming friends with his friends. Yes, I want for you to become one of the guys but you must remember "you are a lady." You must take interest in what they enjoy doing. I want for you to be very laid back and possess the "anything goes" personality. I promise you that once his friends see you to be genuine and think that you are "cool," they will be very accepting of you and will begin to ask about you when you are not around.

One point that I need for you to remember when you are out with his friends— you must be secure and independent! The biggest at ease moment for anyone is to know you can bring a guest to an affair and the guest automatically fits right in.

Here are some tips for you when out with his friends:

1. Always initiate a conversation

2. Never be attached to his hip (Don't make him think he has to entertain you)

Now here is the fun part: becoming friends with his female friends or ex-girlfriends. I know this is blowing your mind and you think I am crazy for adding this but trust me it works! I need for you to be the superior person when you mingle with these ladies. Always take control of the conversation and most of all give a compliment not only to her but to him about her when leaving the event.

So just remember this is a very impressionable time and he needs to see what others truly think of you. So you must be sweet to everyone you meet and never forget the sugar in the kool-aid mix.

After reading this chapter how will you make him yours?

After reading this chapter how will you make him yours?

Chapter 6

Be Salsa! ... Not a block of cheese

This is the **SPICY** chapter!

Ladies, you can have the best personality, be drop-dead gorgeous and have a PH.D, but if you lack sex appeal in bed, you will not keep any man's interest.

If you had to list all your past intimate partners and describe your experiences with each one, I would imagine you would have different comments for each. There were times when you may have been the aggressor in bed and other times when you let him take control. These different experiences are based on your comfort level with each individual. Although I am not a psychologist, I do know that the more comfortable a person feels with their partner, the more sexual they will be with their partner.

I am sure you have heard the saying

"You only have one chance to make a first impression."

I bet many of you have only applied this in your professional life, right? Well, today is a new day so I want you to take that quote and apply it to your SEX life.

Your first sexual encounter with someone new normally sets the pace for all future episodes. So if you are quiet and shy in bed the first time you are intimate, then it will be very hard to become wild and spicy the next time.

I suggest you compare your sex appeal to Salsa. Yes, salsa music is very sexy but I want you to compare your sex appeal to **Salsa dip**! Although, everyone cannot eat spicy food, I need for you to have some type of flavor. Just like salsa —you need to adjust you're your sex appeal to: **Mild, Medium or Spicy!**

In the beginning of this book you learned you must act the role of who you wanted to be to him. Now, I want for you to pick the level of salsa you want to be in bed!

First, think about how you currently are in bed. Now I want for you to kick it up a notch! So if it means watching a porno movie, buying a new wig or sexy lingerie…GO FOR IT!

The trick to having super sex appeal is to actually be all three levels of salsa. Sometimes be mild, most of the time be medium and once a week be SPICY!

What is spicy?

1. A spicy girl is a female that is down for anything and everything. You want sex just as much as he does! You are spontaneous, daring to have intimacy anywhere whether it in a car, under the stars or in a closet.

2. A spicy girl wears lingerie

3. A spicy girl plays the role of different characters

4. A spicy girl enjoys foreplay and tries out the new techniques published in monthly magazines

Most of all, a spicy girl feels comfortable with not only her partner but herself and gives him enough pleasure to keep him coming back. Which, in turn, gives him no reason to go anywhere else.

You know you have succeeded at being a spicy girl when his shyness comes out and you are the one in control in bed.

Here is the catch 20/20: This man is already taken so truthfully you only have 60 days to make him become more interested in you. So I can't tell you when you should become intimate with him. But I do, however, suggest that you shouldn't do it within the first hour of meeting him and I definitely wouldn't wait until the 1439th hour.

Just remember whatever hour you choose, think SALSA! No matter which spice level you decide to choose, never be a "block of cheese." Why? Because cheese is bland and needs something always added to it. Instead, become exciting and be salsa which always is creative and requires water after it!

After reading this chapter how will you make him yours?

After reading this chapter how will you make him yours?

Congratulations!

You are now on your way to becoming an official Man-Snatcher. I hope you have enjoyed this playful book on "How to Make Her Man Yours" and it has made you become more creative in this wonderful world of dating.

Your friend,

Jeanine Michelle
"Ji-Ji"